Beach Bum

Clifton King

Royale Road Publishing

Beach Bum

First Edition
Text font: Times New Roman
Cover design by author

ISBN: 978-0-9786935-6-5

Library of Congress Control Number: 2020912772

Most of these poems were first published, some in different versions, in one or more of the following publications: *San Diego Poetry Annual, Magee Park Poets Anthology, Summation, Perigee, Tidepools,* and in one or more of the author's previous books, *Stolen Afternoons, poetry organic, Street Corner Poet, Confessions of a Poet, sand & water, Beachcombing, Listen to the Tide.*

Printed in the United States of America

Royale Road Publishing, Carlsbad, California

for family, friends and you

Author's note:

Poems in this collection share a common theme: the ocean and its environs, primarily the Southern California coast. So, some similarities exist among the one-hundred plus poems. In fact, there are some instances of different versions of the same poem. Yet, scattered throughout, like seashells on a beach, you will find love, longing, sorrow, death, the healing power of the sea, and the pure joy of just being alive. Their creation spans twenty-five years. They are not in any specific order simply because I can't remember when I wrote which poem. Most have appeared in one, or more, of my previous books of poetry and in other publications as credited on the copyright page. A few are new, making their print debut here.

The sea, once it casts its spell,
holds one in its net of wonder forever.
Jacques Cousteau

Contents

Beach Bum's Lament

The sun has just begun to show
though it is nearly noon.

I watch waves break on shore,
listen to their death rattle,

that final explosion of power
that erodes the very edges of Earth.

Gulls lurk nearby, hoping for a share
of my sandwich. Scattered along the sand,

groups of beachgoers, folding chairs
with built-in umbrellas, beach blankets

held down by huge coolers. A breeze
out of the west whispers life's secrets.

But I don't speak the language,
so catch only a word or two.

Double Overhead

Waves are not measured in feet and inches,
they are measured in increments of fear.
                              Buzzy Trent

Somewhere, in a place as distant
as childhood, storms stir the sea.
Mountains of turquoise and cobalt
rise up like villains in a Grimm fairy tale.

On a morning so bright you forget
it is January, you paddle out
as you have a thousand times before.

Those first dark lines appear on the horizon:
furrows on the forehead of the world.

You race toward them, pray you find refuge
in deep water beyond towering crests,
that silent violence beneath their collapse.

Immortality rides the faces of these waves.
You believe in yourself, call it wisdom,
though from shore it looks like suicide.

You commit, let the sea swallow you
as you stretch a scar of your passage
across her swollen belly.

Life stampedes through your chest.
This is the way you want to die.

I Wander the Beach...

in search of
unbroken seashells.

They are as rare
as unbroken hearts.

I spot one half buried
in the sand.

Closer inspection
reveals an imperfection.

The shell was to be a gift,
a symbol of my love.

Now, this poem will have to do.
This, and every kiss I give you.

Sea Breeze

A sea breeze whispers ashore,
leaves the ocean ruffled with whitecaps,

carves beach sand into ridges & valleys,
gives rise to a lazy line of pelicans,

pulls at the subtle curve of palms
that sway & write your name in the sky.

Venice Beach

Some come to skate or bike
the boardwalk: girls in bikinis
with their slender tan legs;
guys too cool for a shirt,
bodies emblazoned with inked art.
Some come to grunt & sweat
& heft iron in the sand. Thick
necks, rippled abs glisten in the sun.
Some come for beach volleyball
where spikes & full body sacrifices
offer one last chance at fame.
Some come to sit on wooden benches,
watch weirdoes & wait
for the rest of their life to begin.

Love Poems

If my poems were strong enough,
each like the stones Jeffers gathered
along the Carmel coast, I would build
a fortress where I could keep the world
at bay, away from our time together.
I could only hope the rain didn't find
those small crevices between my metaphors.
There would be an English garden out back.
I would paint the garden gate green,
if only for the alliteration.
And beyond the garden, the sea, all blustery
with whitecaps, dappled with the same blue
your eyes smile in the afternoon sun.
And from the forest of words that covers
those distant mountains I would harvest
love poems, lay them in the palm of your hand
                              —along with my heart.

A Morning at Beacon's

The steel guard rail along the bluff
at Beacon's leans toward the sea
a hundred feet below. The earth
is eroding, falling apart, not unlike
today's society, the political system,
justice system, the very fibers
of the American fabric.
There are signs on the guardrail
that warn of a failing bluff, danger.
Again, not so different than
those signs we see every day:
a warning of incompetence,
rambling rants, evidence of ignorance.
I take the trail down to the beach:
a switchback scar on the face
of the bluff, a few wooden steps
here and there. Low tide pushes the sea
back into itself, births a vast expanse
of sand warm from a morning sun.
I walk water's edge, each surge of sea
erases my footsteps, any evidence
I was ever here. Mother Earth struggles
to heal herself. We ignore her cries.

Long Beach State 1961

Sue is a surfer from Ventura.
She has straw colored hair, a smile
that raises my blood pressure. Her
eyes, the color of that seldom seen
green flash, dance when she speaks.
Flawless skin glows a deep tan,
like coffee with too much cream.
A slight smear of pink lipstick
adorns her mouth. We meet most
mornings in the college parking lot;
our token effort at attending classes.
More days than not, we choose now
over the future. My old Chevy
spews blue smoke as we head
for Seal Beach, five miles down PCH.
The campus, perched on a green hillside
with its web of walkways, its halls
of learning, fades in the rear-view mirror,
along with our collegiate careers.

Proposition

Come with me to Paris,
where food is a religion,
love affairs short lived
as clean sheets in a bordello.
I'll buy you the Eiffel Tower
or maybe your own bridge
on the River Seine. We'll stroll
the boulevard, watch artists
struggle with color and light.

But here, in this California
beach town, all I can offer
are craggy coastal bluffs,
a stretch of sand stippled
with impressions of lovers
and the blood of a setting
sun spilled across the sea.
The only Parisian pleasure
I can promise is a French kiss.

Your Name

I spend the morning
at our beach
where the sky
is a collage
of confused clouds,
the ocean dappled
with only a thought
of whitecaps,
and a breeze
that whispers
your name.

Winter Beach

This winter beach mimics
summer. I'm unable to ignore
those women, lithe and lovely,
lying on warm sand, unafraid
to expose pale winter flesh,
flat bellies of youth, thighs
and shoulders smothered
with sunscreen. But soon,
like chameleons that cling
to a setting sun, skin turns
pink, then scarlet, as they
sacrifice themselves for a tan
that will seduce any man.
I consider calling, ask if
you've been outside,
try to decide how to broach
the subject of my interest
       in your tan lines.

Whale Watching

I have come to our beach
to watch for whales.
Those steps down to the sea
are still here—all ninety-four.
But high tides and angry surf
have washed away the sand,
leaving a carpet of cobbles
that glistens when wet,
lies in dry dullness
when baked by the sun.
Beyond the break, where the sea
is smooth with midday glass,
a whale spouts. A wisp of mist
lingers in blue air, then disappears,
not a trace she was ever there.

Day Trip

We cruise Coast Highway.
The Pacific hammers away
at the bluffs on our left.
Off to the right, inland cities,
their mass of humanity,
heat and foul air.

But the California coast
is like a string of pearls;
beach towns too expensive
for our retirement checks;
too chic for your J Jill wardrobe,
my American made car.

Questions for a Friend

Remember those sweet little waves
in La Jolla Cove right in front
of the tennis club; the security guard
who stood on the beach, waved his arms
in the air like a runaway windmill,
tried to tell us we couldn't surf there?
Do you recall how cold the water was
that summer, how clear; and that rock
ledge along the south shore that would
reach up and snag your fin at low tide;
and when the surf was on the rise,
how we slipped into those deep troughs
between rolling mountains of water;
or those calm days when we surfed
that small left under Scripps pier;
and days we paddled up to Black's
where every wave whispered our name?
Remember how warm the car would be after,
how we basked in its greenhouse effect,
traded tales of waves and wipeouts?
I was in La Jolla today, stopped at the Cove.
Everything was much as I remember it:
swimmers out beyond the buoys; groups
of kayakers gawking at leopard sharks
in the shallows; those insistent swells
marching to shore like an invading army.
Yet, I could not recall exactly where
we all paddled out that summer day,
watched your ashes swirl into the deep.

Our Beach

A white belly of moon lingers
in the morning sky, the only
blemish on that pale blue abyss.
A sandpiper's scurry catches my eye,
that race to forage before the next
surge of sea. Above me gulls circle,
call the ocean by name. Sun warms
my shoulders, throws my shadow
down the beach. I hear your voice
in the song of waves, recall that day
you wrote my name in the sand.

Swami's

A remnant of late moon
lingers in the morning sky
even as the sun
    dances on the sea.
Around me, enfolding me,
    the very blood of the earth.

Sea grass bends
and stands straight again.
Dolphins slip past, silent,
    with no concern of me.

Out beyond the edge
where sea and sky fall away
    the stains of a brown haze.

Alas—this is not heaven.

Warm Water

the sea falls away   surging
drawn by the moon   driven
by the wind   beckoning
whispering my name

again and again I return
where afternoon sun paints
the waves   gulls screech
cobbles rattle in the surf

beyond the waves   liquid
shadows flash   rainbows
dance through the mist
of dolphin's breath

pelicans drift on wing
single file   never straight
I stare into the white abyss
of afternoon   searching

for answers along these shores
where billowed sails run before
the wind   silent   unnoticed
like the years of my life

A Morning at Ponto Beach

Pelicans sprawl across a blue collage
of sky, a lazy line unlike those sharp
vees of migrating ducks and geese.

They dip low over the sea, mirrored
in her glassy surface, wing in unison,
then glide—wing, glide—wing, glide.

I wonder if the last in line
calls out the rhythm, the pace,
like a coxswain in a racing shell.

I listen, hear only silence,
that occasional surrender of waves.

Now, the pelicans are gone,
disappeared from sight in the time
it took me to write these few lines,

much the way life slips away
while we are busy with something else.

Wanting You

Sometimes, when my heart aches
I climb that bluff along
Coast Highway, watch the sea,
in whatever mood she might be,
toss waves against shore, white
foam smeared across the sand
        like frosting on a cake.

This morning her waters inky
gray mirror clouds dark enough
to pass as an Oregon sky.
And always the gulls,
        their incessant pleading.

True, there was another
that held my heart for decades
in that mechanical clatter
of pistons and valves, under
the spell of two wheels balanced
between exhilaration and disaster.

At night I dreamt of speed,
blind corners on forest roads,
those last few feet of an unconquered
hillside. But those were years
of a young man unconcerned,
oblivious to his own mortality.

I cannot recall what happened,
which paramour I chased so long
before that time. But now,
well into my seventh decade,
all I want is the sea and a woman.

Interested?

Tsunami
March 11, 2011

Japan quakes with an eight point nine.
And like a rock tossed into a pond,
tsunami waves ripple the sea.
On this side of the world we watch TV,
see a wall of water erase generations.
Killer waves muscle their way around
the globe. The death toll rises like a storm
tide. There is nothing we can do
but offer up a prayer. Life is not fair.
So, I load my board, head for my favorite
surf spot, wait for some tsunami waves.

Tomorrow we mourn the dead.

Beach Girl

I stop at my favorite café, order coffee,
wander out to a sidewalk table
next to a group of old surfers, guys
with skin like leather from all those years
on the water, guys wearing shorts,
sweatshirts, flip flops just as they have
for decades. I settle in with a book
I can't seem to get into. They talk about
swell direction, argue whether Swami's
or Trestles has the best right. They laugh
about John's old truck that threw a rod
on the way to Wind 'n Sea, complain about
the parking meters in Oceanside.
I sense a change in the chatter, peek over
my reading glasses, see a twenty-something
woman at their table. Long sun-bleached
hair falls down her smooth back, skin
luminescent with youth. This is the same
beach girl look I couldn't resist
when we first met. Your blond curls
trying to escape from under that sunhat,
the color of summer painted on your face.
And I knew I wanted to spent the rest of my life
under the influence of your sea-blue eyes.

Omaha Beach
Normandy

today
there is no blood in the sea
no fallen soldiers on the beach
no sniper fire
no incoming rounds
  from battleships
  parked miles off shore
no landing crafts
  overturned in the surf
no enemy machine gun fire
  piercing the air
no cries of *Medic*
no young lives
  seeping into the sand

I cup my hands
raise the cold Atlantic
  to my lips
taste the salt
  of a nation's tears

Beach Talk
Overheard on Carlsbad Blvd

Two young women,
girls really,
push baby strollers
along the beach walk.
They march single file,
a small parade of youth.
Conversation is constant,
animated faces,
arm & hand gestures.
The girl in front,
tall, slender,
sun-bleached hair
pulled tight in a ponytail,
a pair of oversize sunglasses,
a small tattoo
on her shoulder blade,
a fire breathing dragon
hugs her calf,
enough red ink to stop traffic.
And—there is that telltale
baby bump so hard to hide.
They pass my sidewalk bench.
She speaks to her friend
over her shoulder,
All I know is,
I'll never date a surfer again.

A Drive Down PCH

I crest a gentle rise in the road,
and the Pacific greets me
with a blue I've never seen before.
I turn onto Pacific Coast Highway.
My tires slap over each expansion
joint of this old concrete slab roadway.
I'm reminded of days when this
was the only link between San Diego
and my boyhood home in Long Beach.
I recall the overwhelming fragrance
of flower fields, that pungent aroma
of rotting kelp in the summer sun,
this same cadence of tires on concrete.
Carlsbad State Beach, perched atop
an ever-eroding bluff, hugs the highway.
Sinewy coastal shrubs, bent from
the weight of a relentless ocean breeze,
separate campsites. How different
from the Oregon coast where I spent
the seventies and eighties. There,
mountains of old growth fir crawl along
the coastline like a spinney-backed serpent;
the Pacific boils out of control,
not surrendering to breakwaters and jetties
like those that overpower the California coast.
Road noise changes. I realize I've driven past
the beach where I'm to meet my sisters.
I glance at the small silver box on the seat,
Well they can't start without us, can they Dad?

After the Storm

I wander out to the porch
the dogs at my feet.
Morning is still part of the night,
its color that same gray
as the belly of young storm clouds.
Coffee steams in my mug.
Its musky blush reminds me
of that woman, her deep cocoa
skin, eyes dark as a starless night.
But, that's another story
for another time. This morning,
the ocean, just beyond that row
of expensive homes, beckons.
She brings swells alive with power,
swells that have traveled days
across open ocean to be ridden
before dying on these shores,
swells licked into life by a storm
given a name as if it were a newborn
with a lifetime ahead of it.
I finish my coffee, put the dogs
in the house and venture out
to salvage whatever I can
from the remnants of that storm,
whatever its name was.

The ocean fixes everything.

Poet's Perception

I sink into the gray of this first day
of winter, a morning sky streaked
with pale fingers of sunlight.

In this muted chaos pelicans glide
into sight, a great winged string
of beads dropped by an angel.

I watch as they stream above me,
swoop down, skim the sea. Now,
the moment lost—except in memory.

But when the time comes to revisit
this hour with words, the poet's pen
may remember the skies as a woman's

blue eyes and soft smile, while
the string of pelicans will no doubt
become pearls draped about her.

Fish Head

It lies on the carpet of pebbles
a few feet from water's edge,
eye sockets vacant. That thin
layer of scales that once covered
the head, gone, picked clean
by seagulls. Its jaw is clenched
in a grim scowl, small razor-like
teeth exposed, a short section
of backbone with its spiny vertebrae
is still attached. This morning's
high tide may have washed it
ashore, the victim of a hungry seal,
or the discard of a fisherman.
I pick it up, take a few steps
toward the water, toss it
into the sea, back to its beginning.
That is where I want to end,
spend eternity riding the tides.

Surfers aka Shark Bait

Here's an idea. Let's dress up
like a shark's favorite food
and paddle out into the Pacific.
Be sure your wetsuit is black,
that same delicious black
as seal skin, a shark's favorite.
Then, let's kick and splash
around in the open ocean
like an injured or sick sea lion.
Be sure to dangle your feet
off the back of your board
so from deep down in the blue
abyss of the Pacific your silhouette
mimics that of, you guessed it,
a seal, a great white's delight.
But the odds are low that some
razor toothed villain of the deep
will ruin your day, possibly your life.
But then, look at the results
of the 2016 Presidential election.

Exquisite

When I think of *exquisite,* I think of women:
long legs, slender hips, Audrey Hepburn neck,
a walk that says, *Look at me, but don't stare.*
Yet when I think of the beach, *exquisite*
isn't the first word that comes to mind
until I remember a line in a poem I read:
...exquisite as a day at the beach.
Then, images of deserted sand castles,
cloudless skies filled with the cry of gulls,
footprints in wet sand left by lovers with
no destination beyond each other,
that insistent surge of sea, cold swirl
of ocean around your ankles, warm
beach sand beneath a blanket, sun
bright on your face and body as you
offer them up to the tanning God,
give me reason to reconsider.
Long legged women, with their wonderful
walk; a day at the beach. Yes, exquisite.

November Observation
surfer's lament

Morning sun on my face
Dismal clouds sweep in from the west
    warmth siphoned off
    by a harsh chill
    hiding in that brooding sky
Coffee still warm in my cup
I gaze across an endless reach of sea
    where meaningless swells
    roll off the horizon
Nothing suggests I abandon my coffee
    paddle out

Flight

Sky stretches
lifeless
horizon to horizon.
Lines of Pelicans
that filled these skies
yesterday, now
lines on the poet's page.
Words in flight
journey
margin to margin,
destination
known only
to the poet.

Down to the Sea
For David Martin, killed by a great white, April, 2008

David Martin is lifted from the sea
like a man pulled from the submersion
of baptism, soul offered up to God,
a sacred sacrament of surrender.

Why is David the chosen one?
Is it the shape his body makes in the ocean,
a silhouette so similar to a sea lion,
maybe mistaken for a sick struggling seal?

Questions that remain unanswered
as the Great White rushes toward the surface,
ghost like lids closed over cold black eyes,
jaws agape, row upon row of serrated teeth exposed.

David Martin cries out the name of his God
as he is heaved from ocean waters
into the chilly morning air, his blood
staining the sea, before being dragged below,
the Pacific drowning his screams.

There will be no triathlon, no celebration
of his personal victory, no finisher's tee-shirt,
no trophy, no photos, no plans for the next event.

The waters off Solana Beach roil
with the thrashing of arms and legs,
caudal and dorsal fin—then silence.
The Great White has realized her mistake.
Yet, there are no apologies as she swims
out to sea still in search of her next meal.

A flotilla of primordial instincts dwells
just off shore, and those of us
who go down to the sea—pray for God's mercy.

Once again…

it begins with a gray smudge of sky
& meaningless swells
mounting in the west
on a green blanket of ocean
& the mirrored flight of Pelicans
in silent revelry.

Greener Days

A lone tree stands
on a bluff above the Pacific.
Bent from the constant caress
of an ocean breeze,
branches bare, stark
against an ever-changing coastal sky,
not a single leaf or bud
with the promise of new life.
When I was a younger man
it was green with creation
and threw shade across
purple blossoms that crowded
the ground around it.
I would unfold my beach chair,
sit in its shadow, write poetry,
never a thought of that tree
becoming nothing more
than deadwood, or of me
growing into an old man
remembering greener days.

Indian Beach

A slice of wild Oregon coast,
wide, windswept,
dotted with tide pools.
Sea stacks
rise from the ocean.
We travel the road in,
long and winding,
meandering
beneath a canopy
of coast range forest
thick with evergreens,
carpeted in ferns.
Offshore,
Tillamook Rock Lighthouse
still stands guard
in an oft angry sea.
And in a light spring rain
I kiss her the first time.

Boy Chasing Birds

A boy chases gulls down the beach.
His stride ungainly, spindly legs
like a young colt. He tosses cobbles
harvested from wet sand exposed
by a minus tide. His arm, his aim
hold no promise of a MLB career.
His father shouts, *Don't throw rocks.*
Seagulls light farther down the beach.
Perhaps expecting compliance.
But the boy gathers more cobbles.
And soon, gulls take flight.

Watercolor

A watercolor hangs on the gallery wall.
Liquid sunlight falls through
frenzied palm fronds. Dappled shadows
creep across white cabanas. A group
of men walk on a black sand beach,
their gaze out toward a hazy horizon.
I want to know what those men
are looking at, where they are going.
I imagine myself in the painting,
feel warm sand beneath my feet,
midday sun hot on my shoulders.
Out beyond small breakers
a woman struggles
in the deep blue of depression,
her cries muted by mouthfuls
of sea green. I hear God's name
in her pleading, in panic that will
not keep her afloat. Has she
changed her mind about drowning
her failures. And who is that man
in the blue shirt, her lover, a friend?
I have the perfect place for this piece.
But will I hang only the rustle of palms,
skies filled with threatening clouds,
men out for a walk on the beach?
Or, am I going to hear that woman's cries
every time I step into the room?

Fall

Leaves do not turn and fall
here along the California coast
like in New England. We don't
have to rake that kaleidoscope
of demise into small mounds
for ceremonial disposal later.

Our highways are not littered
with yellow and orange that
take flight with every passing car.
We don't have those skeletal
silhouettes scratching the belly
of gray winter skies.

But once you stand on a beach
ankle deep in the ocean, watch
the sun kiss a waiting horizon,
then drown itself in the sea,
you will know the beauty
of a New England fall
            is not God's best work.

Storm Warning

A purple silhouette of Oceanside Pier,
that massive finger of Dana Point
consume the horizon like an invading army.
Yet, the sea does not surrender. Not to them
nor those *Devil Winds* that sweep in
with their dry desert breath. Even the sailor
doesn't understand the whims of this woman:
how swiftly her mood morphs when wind
whispers secrets we cannot comprehend;
when sunlight, sudden as a lightning strike,
changes her into liquid chrome and she
lures the unwary far from safe shores.
So, all who answer her call, beware.
The sea can be as dangerous as a love affair.

When it is done…

let me slip beneath the sea,
plunge to her depths
                              and rest,
my flesh for the scavengers,
never to be in the earth,
                              bones in a box,
covered over and trampled upon.

Glorious repose,
forever in the thunder of waves.

January 20, 2020
surfer's lament

The morning sea is stormy
with whitecaps and chop,
cold as an Arctic flow.
A gray streaked sky
presses down, holds
this frigid January air captive.
A slant of sunlight forces
through a distant break,
lays a luminous silver swath
across the ocean with only
an illusion of warmth.
There is little reason to paddle out,
every reason to just be here.

Baptism

Morning rises, rumpled and gray,
like an old man from a restless sleep.
The constant concert of waves washes
the shore clean like God granting
absolution to the earth. This beach,
as close to heaven as I may ever get.

The years have tempered my desire
to be anointed in the roll and tumble
of white water, held up to the high priest
of accomplishment on each crest.

Yet, I cannot commit myself to the safety
of the sidewalk, alone, with only memories
to fill my hours. As a believer
I need the sun's warmth on my face,
that daily baptism in the Pacific.

Beachcombing Bounty

I save you a slice of summer sun,
a few grains of beach sand,
pack it all away in a shell
I find half buried by the sea,
the blood of high tide still shiny
on those ringed ridges of its back.
There is a necklace of kelp
tangled and knotted along shore.
But you are not one for jewelry.
So, I leave it for the incoming tide
or those children chasing seagulls.
I gift you my beachcombing bounty
as if it holds some value.
Your smile confirms what I knew
from the beginning:
the sea, with her unpredictable sky,
is no longer my first love.

Ashes
— for Jeff

Tomorrow, when I see the new blue
of morning sky, feel sun on my face,
I will think of you old friend,
all those hours we spent watching
the horizon, waiting on that perfect
wave, holding on to life.
And then breakfast at The Deli:
coffee, bacon and eggs seasoned
with stories of long-ago travels;
afternoons in your living room,
dogs sprawled on the couch, and you
content in that canine clutter. But
your trips to the hospital scared the hell
out of me. How I admired your courage.
So tomorrow, when I see that new
morning sky, feel the sun's warmth,
I will think of those last minutes
I spent with you old friend:
that day in La Jolla Cove when we
let you go, a swirl of ashes, a spirit
who couldn't wait to return to the sea.

Cadence

Seduced by the sea, by a wind out of the west,
I stand smooth curve of tiller in hand.
A lover's rhythmic cadence rising on the crest

she shudders beneath me, deck awash in our quest.
A belly of white canvas sail I command,
seduced by the sea, by a wind out of the west.

I cling to her, man at earth's bountiful breast,
then rejoice, each thrust of bow grand,
a lover's rhythmic cadence rising on the crest.

She flies, wind across her beam, reaching, pressed
against clouds and empty sky traced in the sand.
Seduced by the sea, by a wind out of the west

I believe her whispered promise, safe harbor's rest,
sails lowered in the blushing beauty of her land.
A lover's rhythmic cadence rising on the crest

spills sailors and Captain into a sea of confessed
desire. There they surrender to her hand,
seduced by the sea, by a wind out of the west,
and a lover's rhythmic cadence rising on the crest.

Addiction

That weekend chaos on Pacific Coast Highway rumbles
passed as I stand at the edge of a bluff above the Pacific.
Below, a thread of beach stretches along the California coast.
It is overrun by the multitudes escaping inland heat.
The vivid reds, blues and greens of beach umbrellas
and sunshades smear the sand with a collage of color
like an impressionist painting. This façade disappears
into that distant haze regurgitated from the LA basin.
The ocean today is lake-like, calm, well mannered,
nearly silent where sea meets sand. The pungent
aroma of rotting, fly infested, seaweed mingles
with the sweet scent of sunscreen and hibachi smoke.
Small children at water's edge scream and laugh
with the pure joy of cold ocean water swirling
around their ankles. Most men and women on the beach
are attired in swimwear they really should reconsider.
But I'm not here to judge. I'm here for my ocean fix.
I take a hit of sea breeze, drop a little summer sky,
mainline this late June sun and that lazy line of pelicans.

Compassion

He stands on the walkway along Carlsbad's seawall,
beard and hair unkempt, but not frighteningly so.

He has that sunburned face of a man who spends
most of his time outside, on the streets, homeless.

Bedroll over his shoulder he leans into the shadow
of lifeguard tower 22. He stares out at the ocean,

maybe thoughts of better days, or maybe just a stare.
There is no way to know his story, what brought him

here, where he came from. But a man fifty feet
down the walk is afraid of what he doesn't know.

He is on his cell phone talking with the police.
He will probably take a picture, post it on social media,

brag about how he helped clean up the neighborhood.
I continue my walk, wonder when compassion died.

January Beach Walk

The sand beneath my feet
is damp with remnants
of high tide. The sky
is an apricot umbrella,
sun just over the horizon.
I reach out to take
your hand, interlock
our fingers so we
will never be apart.
But there are only
my footprints in the sand
and this January air
is cold in my empty hand.
The gulls call your name,
or is that just me?

Ponto Jetties

A rusty bicycle leans against the railing
on Batiquitos Lagoon bridge. Nearby,
an old man tosses bread crumbs into the air.
Seagulls swarm in the cold morning sky,
scurry about stealing food from each other.
He speaks to them, calls several by name.
I can't tell one seagull from another.
He is a short man, wears a dirty sports jersey
with the number nineteen emblazoned across it.
A braid of gray hair dangles down his back.
Unruly tufts peek out from under his cap.
A matted mass of beard covers his face.
Bread crumbs gone, he bids farewell
to the gulls. Half-way across the bridge
he leans over the rail, shouts something,
then peddles off. I walk out on the bridge,
peer over the rail. Nothing but lagoon water
rushing out to sea with the receding tide.
What am I missing?
Is it something the seagulls said to him?

Aloha

We came home with tall tales
of the North Shore of Oahu:
Pipeline, Sunset Beach, Waimea Bay.
Wide-eyed surfers believed every word

about the North Shore of Oahu,
seldom surfed in those early days.
Wide eyed surfers believed every word
about that far-away, unattainable Mecca.

Seldom surfed in those early days,
those old-style logs not up to the task
in that far-away, unattainable Mecca.
Hawaii beckoned, Barbers Pt. to Diamond Head.

Those old-style logs not up to the task
at Pipeline, Sunset Beach, Waimea Bay.
Hawaii beckoned, Barbers Pt. to Diamond Head
and we came home with tall tales.

Live in the sunshine, swim in the sea,
drink the wild air...
Ralph Waldo Emerson

Warm Water Jetty 2019

The wind is out of the north, gusting cold.
I wander the bluff above the sea at Terra Mar.
There is a waning swell from last week's storm.
A few surfers bob randomly in the ocean,
stare at the horizon. But the super tide pushes
every wave to shore before allowing it to break.
I work my way down to the beach where
Warm Water Jetty used to jut into the surf
just south of the power plant outflow.
Now, only a skeleton of boulders remains.
I find one that provides a protected perch,
its surface rough and warm. This black basalt
boulder has memorized the afternoon sun.
The sea forces its way up a cobbled slope,
turns, rushes back into itself. The ocean roars
with the frenzy of pebbles dragged out to sea.
I sit alone in this place awash in memories.
It was 1963 when I first came to this beach.
Jimmy and I drove down from Lakewood,
two balsa boards tied to the roof of his Vee Dub.
We parked along the bluff, long before a seawall
and the parking lot at Tamarack. Twenty-six
years later I returned and called it home.
This is the beach where I met Jeff and Rob
one Saturday morning in '93. This beach
where, for decades, we shared friendship,
the waves and our love for the ocean.
Jeff is gone now. He used up those twelve
extra years his heart-transplant bought him.
Rob moved to Oregon a decade ago. For years
I've come to sit on the jetty, listen to the waves.
Now, the jetty is gone, like many friends
and a few family. But listen, do you hear that?
The sea still has stories to tell.

Humpbacks

Out beyond the silver wash of sand
Below those blue green ripples of life
Gray shadows slip past unnoticed

Terra Mar

I barely set foot on the sand when that pungent odor of rotting seaweed engulfs me, sweeps me away like a rogue wave back to my childhood where every day smelled of decaying kelp and Coppertone sun tan lotion, the legacy of all who lived in a Southern California beach town, those small communities clinging to PCH like life itself depended on it, towns scattered along that ribbon of asphalt like a string of pearls draped around the slender neck of the Southern California coast, Manhattan, Redondo and Palos Verdes, Seal Beach, Huntington, San Clemente, Oceanside, Del Mar, La Jolla and PB, where life taught you respect for the ocean, her many moods, that sway of the moon, earth's rotation, whitecaps born of a far off storm, spindrift dancing in the sky, unseen currents stirred by Neptune's scepter, and in those early years you went with questions, expected to find answers in bits of broken shells, that mystical glide of pelicans, a tangle of seaweed strewn on the sand, and you listened to her voice late at night, at times angry with the distant thunder of her breakers, or nearly silent, so subdued you dressed, went down to the shore to quell your fears that somehow those dark waters had evaporated into the shadowy night, spilled over the horizon. But for those who love her, the sea is always there.

Coming Home

I was born on a beach
just beyond the reach
of high tide. Yet,
I have not always been
a neighbor of the sea.
In those years that survived
my youth, mountains,
the color of freedom, bled rivers
into the valleys of my dreams.
And the same rain that fell
on ancient conifer forests
nourished the Oregon lifestyle.
But I was born on a beach
and have returned like
a spawning salmon
to end where I began.

First Beach Walk in Two Months
May 4, 2020

This morning the sun shines
a brilliant white in a pale
eastern sky. Yet, fog huddles
against the coastline,
a damp curtain over the sea.
An undecipherable prophecy.
I fill a thermos with coffee,
a survival kit of sorts, head
for the beach. Fletcher Cove.
The parking lot closed,
taped off like a crime scene.
But foot traffic is allowed:
exercise only; don't stop;
don't stand around; wear a mask.
What the sign means is,
Don't let COVID-19 catch you.
Think of how safe life would be
on the Serengeti if the zebra,
water buffalo and gazelle
were given such a warning.
Don't stop. Don't stand around.
Think of the lioness's frustration,
the hunger in her pride's belly.
I pull on my mask, check
over my shoulder for that nasty
COVID-19 and start down the beach.
A red tide laps at the sand.
The surf is small, inconsistent,
yet a few of the foolish venture
into the algae soup. A stink
hangs in the air, replacing
the early morning fog.
And it looks as if everyone
has just pulled off a bank robbery.
But—what a glorious walk.

Normandy on My Mind

We walk the beach
south of Cardiff.
A minus tide reveals
a stretch of sand
reminiscent
of Omaha Beach.
But this beach
doesn't have
the history
or the blood stains.

Lover

She is here, waiting,
where I last left her.
I touch her, she me,
for the first time in months.
We have been together
for a lifetime—my lifetime.
She was there in the beginning:
And the Spirit of God
was hovering over
the face of the waters.
Her names are as many
as the stars. Yet, I have
only known her as the Pacific.
This name, from the Latin
pacificus. Peaceful.
She welcomes me back,
doesn't ask where I have been
as I immerse myself in her
peaceful liquid embrace.

Another Day at the Office

It's been years since that clutter of desk,
inane babble around the coffee pot
in a windowless tomb of capitalism.

Now, my office is the edge of the sea,
sand warm beneath bare feet. No one
to meet except the incoming tide.

On the sand, remnants of the weekend:
plastic pails, Tupperware tubs
and towering turrets of sandcastles.

I park along the curb where rusted relics
of Detroit iron regurgitate a semi-melodic
ruckus; where tattooed young men

and guys gray with time gather
for our morning ritual in the waves.
Just another day at the office.

February Whale Watching

The bluff where I stand is scarred
by eons of wind and stormy seas.
The Pacific is dappled with whitecaps.
Above it, an angry sky, threatening clouds.
A north wind bites at my face.
A woman on the beach, her pant legs
rolled up to mid-calf but wet
well above her knees, picks up a shell,
examines it, then tosses it into the sea.
Barefoot, she steps gingerly
on a blanket of beach cobbles,
ropes of kelp rotting along shore.
Her dog, a yellow Lab, runs free,
chases gulls, dashes franticly
in and out of the whitewater.
Two days ago, I saw four
California Grays from this bluff.
Their massive backs glistened
in the sun when they surfaced,
spouts hung in the air,
an announcement
ghost-like against a blue sky.
Today, no shiny arched backs,
not a single blow on the horizon.
Yet, the beauty of sea and sky
is no less. If only you were here.

Ashes of Life
after the California wildfires

The sea, calm as a sleeping child,
mirrors the skimming glide of pelicans.
A gull's cry pierces morning air
and I'm lost in the sun's warmth.

Offshore, a lone lobster boat.
A man on deck checks his catch.
I cannot see his face but know his
disappointment with each empty trap.
It has not been a good season.

Beyond the boat, a horizon tinted
with a brown ghost of smoke
from wildfires, those hazy remains
of scrub pine, willows and eucalyptus;
ranch style homes and barns, stables
and corrals, small summer cottages
and weekend shacks; everything
those flames exhaled
      after taking in all there was.

The lobster boat moves on.
And somewhere, in distant canyons,
along lonely ridges,
people sift through the ashes of life.

Boy at the Beach

He picks up a stone,
its flat face as smooth

as his own, and takes aim
at a flock of resting gulls.

Their instant flight
a tight circle
in the December air.

They settle back in,
danger past.

Down the beach, the boy
searches for another stone.

California Gray

What has drawn her into the channel
at Agua Hedionda lagoon?
Her barnacled body struggles,
rolls on its side, flipper exposed
at an odd angle, like the sail
of a boat adrift on a stormy sea.
She labors to recover & surface
for a breath. Every wave disrupts
her progress. There is no power
in the sweep of her mighty tail.
People crowd the jetties,
line the highway bridge.
A hundred iPhones capture
the moment. Three girls
joke as they try for a selfie,
whale in the background.
Children, atop their fathers' shoulders,
laugh & shout in that shrill voice
of youth. A guy, on his phone,
explains to his girlfriend why he'll be late.
The Gray slips under the highway bridge.
The outflow carries her back
down the channel toward the sea.
She begins her struggle anew,
rolls onto her side & sinks.
Her long, slender shape
a dark scar on the white sand bottom.
But the crowd has lost interest.
Only a few remain to witness the end.
There is nothing to be done,
like the morning my mother died
—within reach, but beyond help.

After Labor Day

Summer lowers
into autumn
and September
surrounds us.
That flowing
sweep of sand
lies naked
as sand castles
and footprints
are erased
by the tide,
forgotten
by the hordes
of yesterday.
Gulls huddle
against the wind,
sandpipers dance
near water's edge.
The pledge of fall
paints a purple sky
and once again
we are free to be
alone with friends.

Black's

Out of the northeast
a murmur of summer wind
this December day.

The sea, silent beneath
towering cliffs of opulence,
awakens,

rises from the depths
as beguiling emerald walls
pleading for our touch.

Believer

In this lazy beach town,
just north of that chaotic
Mexican border,
there is a set of stairs
down to the sea.

On the fragile face
of this bluff a drape
of passionate purple
blooms: a native plant
whose name escapes me,
if I ever did know it.

On a good day
storm swells march in,
collide with a shallow reef
just off shore, shoot skyward.
A perfect wave some say.

I sit silently in my truck,
sip hot coffee and wait.
I have faith in the forecast
of a coming south swell,
just as mankind clings
to the hope of heaven.

Healing

I sit in the shade
of a gnarled coastal pine
this summer look-alike
November day.
A line of pelicans
stitches clouds to sky
above sea scarred
bluffs of Del Mar.
The bite of rotting kelp,
sweetness of sunscreen,
and ocean mist memories
fill my afternoon.

December 22, 2017
Ponto Jetties

The air is December cold,
the sea, slate gray.
A small swell sweeps down
from the northwest.
Morning sunshine shimmers
on the face of each wave
before it spills over onto itself.
Two days from now will mark
the beginning of my seventy-fifth year,
decades of flirting with the tides,
the many moods of an uncertain sea.
I wander out onto the granite architecture
that is the north jetty, amazed
that man still believes he can control
the ocean, dictate her behavior.
Seagulls feast on mussels exposed
by a low tide. That vast expanse
of beach created by a retreating sea
will disappear in a matter of hours
as the tide turns. I consider paddling out,
allow the sea to consume me.
In her embrace I am a young man;
the world, anything I can imagine.

A Drive Up Pacific Coast Highway

Vacant balconies jut from multi-million-dollar homes.
Empty patio chairs, gas grills hidden beneath dusty
covers stand silent as barbeque utensils rust in ocean air.
But I don't see a single person. I never do. So, where are
the people who first stepped onto these decks,
saw the sparkle of sun on the Pacific, heard the ocean's
voice welcome them to the neighborhood? Did they stay
long enough to see the spectacle of November's red sunsets;
listen to the laugh of gulls; feel those wisps of morning fog
creep ashore; watch an informal formation of pelicans
stitch clouds to the sky? Or was it always about resale value?
What a shame, blinded by a few coins of the realm.

When I'm Gone

I'll miss
that never-ending march
of waves, beach cobbles
and those blood red sunsets
that whisper promises
to the horizon.

I'll miss
the musical poetry
of our Soleri wind-bell
in an easy ocean breeze,
broken sea shells
and the glide of pelicans
above indifferent waters.

I'll miss
that smell of kelp
washed ashore
by last night's high tide,
warm sand beneath my feet
and those late moons
that linger in a morning sky.

I'll miss
the cry of gulls
scavenging on the beach,
those summer showers
that leave a rainbow behind
and I'll miss the hot summer sun.

But when I'm gone,
and the memory of me
is scattered
along the California coast,
I'll miss you the most.

Surfing *Grandview*

I hadn't expected much.
It seems to get in the way,
expecting, then not receiving.
But I had reason.
Thick gray clouds smeared
the morning sky, the breath
of a distant storm swept
the ocean into a frenzy.

Yet, two cups of coffee later
sunlight fell from the sky,
the slightest suggestion
of whitecaps danced
on a now sparkling sea.

I hadn't expected much,
certainly not walls of green water
towering over dark troughs;
explosions of white,
violent and unforgiving;
fear and sweet satisfaction.

Tide Pool

An Egret stands statue-like
atop a small spire of beach rock,
white plumage stark against a denim sky.
In a shallow hollow of sand, a sea star
lies stranded by the retreating ocean.
It will be hours before the tide turns.
This is nature's way. There is no blame
to be placed. Yet, you feel obligated
to return this creature to deeper waters.
Nearby, half a mussel shell, remnants
of seagulls foraging. The shell is slender,
slightly scooped, perfect for your needs.
You slip it under the creature's belly,
carry her to the deepest edge of the tide pool.
As she sinks slowly to the bottom
one of her arms moves ever so slightly.
A *Thank You* wave?

Boneyard
observations from a kayak

I paddle into the morning cold,
fog following the night into the west,
a breeze off the sea cool against my skin.
Yellow comes the sun
painted on a pale canvas of morning sky.
Its warmth: the embrace of an old friend,
                              a lover's kiss.

Somewhere, a storm licks at the sea,
pushes her away sending swells marching,
hundreds, thousands of miles
to rise up, then tumble and die.
The murmur of waves: words whispered
                    that go straight to the heart.

Beyond the surf, a flotilla of kelp
heaving with the ebb, alive with shorebirds
and black-eyed seals.
On the distant shore a train rumbles,
sounds a long blast, then falls silent.

Now —
        only the croak of a Cormorant,
        the tremolo call of the Loons
        and the water dripping off my paddle
        rippling the transparent world below.

La Jolla Cove

We reach into summer
from these last days of December
& journey placid waters,

drift through kelp beds
rising from the green broth,
& surrender to the ebb.

From a tangle of brown leaves
wide eyed seals
question our intentions.

Caves & craggy points
below crumbling bluffs
testify to the rage of wind & sea.

We linger
near the edge of humanity,
the masses within sight.

Reluctant to return
we wait for that silence
of heaven's half-light.

One with the Pacific

After recent high tides and strong surf
the California coast is a ribbon of cobble
embankments that rattles as each wave
clamors ashore. I do the *rock dance*
across cobbles down to water's edge.
The Pacific pulses around me, water
cool, but not as cold as the Atlantic
that day I waded in at Omaha Beach.
I stand at the edge of the earth.
Every wave that washes over my feet
sucks sand back out to sea. Soon
I am buried ankle deep, entrenched,
rooted in the sea like a California kelp.
Once again, I am one with the Pacific.

Surf Check at *Old Man's*

I pull to the edge of the bluff,
switch off the ignition.
Merle Haggard is replaced
with the music of water
collapsing on itself,
waves birthed in far-off seas
by mystical elements of nature:
wind, fetch, bottom contours
& King Neptune's mood.
The morning air is uneasy
with a *Devil Wind*.
Spindrift peels from wave tops.
Today, giants roll in
twice the height of a tall man.
Double overhead is the proper term.
Fear & respect is the proper approach.

To the Sea

— for Jeff

Beyond this barren stretch
of sand, beyond that chaos
of white water, out where waves
are born, your spirit still lives.

We returned you to the sea
just as you asked old friend.
The sea—the only place
you ever wanted to be.

Storm

There is that moment
when wind first finds the sea,
sweeps down & licks
at her liquid curves;
that moment when
the birth of a storm
is still in doubt,
whitecaps unimagined,
that turbulent mix
of cobalt & turquoise
only a possibility.
But if the sea surrenders
to these overtures,
which she almost always
does, there is a tempest
no man can tame,
only hope to survive
as cannon shots of thunder
& lightning strikes
make you wonder
if Ben Franklin
is somewhere in the clouds
flying his kite.

If you're lucky enough
to live by the sea,
you're lucky enough.

Mid-Morning at Ponto Beach

I went beachcombing today.
The sea restless, somewhat upset by a far-off storm.
A torrent of water rushed between Ponto jetties
as low tide tried to empty Batiquitos Lagoon.
Broken shells littered the shore.
The sand still dark, damp from yesterday's rain.
Two women wandered water's edge, inspecting cobbles
before dropping them into shopping bags.
A young girl walked a dog down to the water,
turned it loose to chase seagulls.
I looked for a heart shaped cobble or a piece of driftwood
I could bring home to you, but found only those bits
of broken shells I mentioned.
But you know the best thing about beachcombing?
After I've filled my lungs with sea air,
listened to a hundred waves break,
felt the sun on my face,
I get to come home to you.

Late in the Season

I park on the bluff along PCH,
tune in an *oldies* radio station;
watch the morning sea,
gray as those clouds
that cling to the bottom of the sky.
Only a hint of green in small swells
that stand up, then collapse on the sand.
In the distance, whale spouts.
Mother and calf.
The long arc of her back
glistens in early light.
It's late in the season
for returning whales.
On the radio, *Come Go With Me.*
The Dell Vikings from 1957.
I recall sock hops in the gymnasium,
a girl named Anita
and smoking Luckies
stolen from my dad's pack.
I notice the whales are gone now,
just like those sock hops
and that girl.
Late in the season, indeed.

Divine Disclosure

The ocean gives up her bones.
Small shards of shells, the color
of moonlight, litter the shore;
smooth to the touch, weightless
as summer sun in your hand.
I harvest a few wedged among
cobbles still damp from high tide.
The beach is an unmarked canvas
from last night's rain. I shake
pieces of shells in cupped hands,
spill them onto the sand
like a Voodoo bone reader.
Their pattern reveals a secret.
They would speak to a real diviner.
What could they possibly say to me?
Maybe—the reasons I love you.
But I don't need bits of shells
to tell me what I already know.

Ode to October

October is morning fog that drives fair weather
beach goers back to their cottages for daytime TV;
a swell sweeping down out of the north, the crash of surf
on shore, waves giving themselves to the earth
like lovers behind closed doors; long lines of pelicans
skimming wave tops; low tides that leave mirrors
in the sand where you can step on the sky.

October is when you notice that couple from a timeshare
down the road; their borrowed beach towels;
plump, white bodies sampling the cold Pacific
before their flight back to Grand Rapids.

October in Southern California is not about that first
dusting of snow; the scramble to find tire chains and bags
of rock salt somewhere in the basement; discovering
the snow shovel has a broken handle; nor the frightening
realization that you forgot to order heating fuel for winter.

October in Southern California is a time to rejoice.
October is our savior, our redemption from a summer
overrun with tourists and no surfing after eleven.

Surf Safari

In the cab of my truck, coffee cup cradled
between my hands, steam streaks the windshield.
Outside, the Pacific pounds against a beach I knew
in my childhood. I have returned, not through
some portal in the space time continuum,
not beamed here by a Star Trekish transporter,
rather by a simple drive up Coast Highway.

I unload my board and make that long walk
across sand already hot from the morning sun,
across sand I have crossed a hundred times,
across sand marked with the footprints of my youth.

I step into the sea and paddle into the past,
out through waves of memory, where
fear was an unknown word, where we knew
there would always be a tomorrow.

In this cold water I wait for swells
to build, sun warm on my bare shoulders,
on my skinny sixteen-year-old frame. Friends
nearby laugh and talk that nonsense of youth.

Finally, frigid waters take their toll. We head
for the beach to huddle in the sun, lie about
those great waves we caught, whistle at girls,
throw sand and be young.

I feel a tug on my shoulder, turn to look
into the face of an old man—my surf buddy.
Wake up, he insists. *We can still catch
the senior special breakfast at Denny's.*

Shorebird

Her small skeleton still intact
she lies on the cobbles
just above high tide line.
A few feathers still adorn her
hollow bones, tiny beak
on her long straight neck
like the head of a spear.
I don't see her legs or feet.
Scavengers have finished
with her, tiny carcass
now baking in the sun.
She is weightless
in the palm of my hand,
no smell of death,
remains delicately rigid.
I leave her where I found her
just as they left Mallory
where they found him on Everest.

Life's Sidewalk

A March wind out of the west
dapples the sea with whitecaps.
Coastal wildflowers bow their heads
in a dance of purple and yellow.
The sky is a monochrome canvas
of slate blue. Gulls glide above
the bluff, ride invisible waves
of the cloudless morning air.
A young Egret swoops in,
begins her hunt for lizards
along the craggy bluff's edge.
In the green undergrowth
a squirrel burrows in the earth.
A lone surfer steps from the sea,
walks along the sidewalk.
Wet footprints mark his path.
They soon dry and disappear.
I've watched the footprints
of my children's childhood fade
into memories; the footprints
of my parent's lives ebb
on a tide that never returned.
Now, at seventy-five,
I check over my shoulder
to see if my footprints are fading
from life's sidewalk.

Beyond Tidewater…

a meld of kayaks and ocean.
The slow tolling of a buoy bell
announces the cadence of a rising sea.

On the distant shore, immorality
prejudice and greed lie in wait.
Weeds among the wildflowers.

So, we linger, enraptured by the bark
of a sea lion, swooping flight of pelicans
and friendship's silence.

At Our Beach

I sit with sun on my face,
realize the glow I feel
comes from my thoughts of you.

I wonder how long
I've given the sun credit
for the warmth of your love?

Seashells

I walk water's edge,
wet sand cool beneath bare feet.
In the distance,
the rumble of Coast Highway.
But the song of the sea, waves
breaking on shore, comforts me.
I scan the sand for unbroken shells,
a gift to give my love.
When I was a child wandering
the shores of Seal Beach
high tide would often carpet
the sand with perfect sea shells.
There were as many shells as stars,
as many shells as days in a lifetime.
Today, I find only one unbroken shell.

Ponto Beach
second day of 2019

A January breeze persuades me to slip on a sweatshirt.
The sea sparkles with sunlight. Wispy lines of whitewater
streak its surface. A couple walks at water's edge, barefoot,
pants rolled up. The cold ocean swirls around their ankles.
A small child scurries down the beach, tries to tease
her kite into flight. A dog runs loose on the sand. Seagulls
sit atop wooden poles that hold up volleyball nets.
I stuff my hands deep into my sweatshirt pockets. The sky
is a cloudless slate blue that morphs to silver white
at that razor-sharp line where sea and sky meet. Meager
morning surf beckons half a dozen surfers. With every surge
of sea, the rattle of cobbles. I step up onto the north jetty:
granite chunks the size of a child's bed, blasted from
some distant mountain; laid with such precision, top so flat
you can walk as easily as strolling down Coast Highway.
At jetty's end I sit, face south so the wind is at my back,
sun on my face. Near me an old man fishes in the channel
between the jetties. My father was a fisherman. He told
stories of my mother and him fishing the Sea of Cortez, their
small aluminum boat, a stray cat they fed while cleaning fish,
that rusty water tank, those decades they had together.
                    Now, they have eternity.

Thursday Morning Thoughts

Through my open door I look down our street
toward the Pacific, slender palms stark against
a cloudless morning sky, that faux horizon
of those red tile rooftops of multi-million-dollar
homes. I hear waves attacking the bluffs
along Carlsbad Boulevard, that occasional
train whistle, Marine helicopters cruising
the coast serious about their war games.
My second cup of coffee sits on the desk,
steam rising from that dark elixir
the way I imagine magic vapors materialized
from Aladdin's lamp. I take a sip, make a wish.

Fog begins to roll in. Sandburg wrote:
it comes on little cat feet. This fog muscles
its way ashore like a bull. Damp air edges
its way through the door, the way an open
refrigerator spills cold onto the floor.

I'm reminded of motorcycle rides in the fog:
the early sixties in Seal Beach, a summer's
evening ride south along PCH to Huntington,
or inland to visit a girl I knew in Buena Park.
I'd fly along wrapped in the comfort of youth,
nothing more than a tee shirt and Levi's
to shield me from the night. Fog lay in hollows,
in open spaces that have long since disappeared.
It reached out, grabbed hold until my bones rattled.

Now, I sip my coffee, notice the fog has lifted.
That's life along the coast, life everywhere:
look away for a minute—everything changes.

La Jolla Shores

we venture beyond trivial waters
to the distant rising of the sea
where giants march toward shore
and lift us to the sky

Questions

I wonder about the seagulls.
How do they know when
a minus tide will expose
mussels that cling
to these jetty boulders?
Do they read the same
tide charts I do?
And when did they learn
to open those shells
held together as tightly
as a child's hands in prayer?

Old Man Sitting on the Seawall

She ran off with another man.
Not that I can really blame her,
all those years I spent chasing waves
in Costa Rica, Hawaii and Mexico,
never home long enough to see
she was drifting away, that I was
losing the only woman I ever loved.
That's not true of course. The sea
has always been my first love.
You see those waves behind me,
perfectly shaped, as if an artist
painted them. That's what I lived
for, that was the shape that drove
me insane the way the curve
of a woman's leg, the line
of her neck or small of her back
can push a man over the edge.
But my time is over.
I had decades of that love affair,
caressed by the sea, summer sun
whispering life's secrets. But I heard
only what I wanted and refused
to see the truth. Now, I have only
my memories and this wall where
I sit and watch as my lover embraces
the young man I once was.

You Call My Name

Seal Beach, California, summer of '46.
I play at water's edge, fearless, wade in
too deep, feel the pull of the Pacific.
Mother, you call my name, reach for me,
your hands strong with love.

Now, I walk barefoot in the shallows.
The sea swirls cool against my skin.
Overhead, a lazy line of pelicans
drifts by in a stormy sky.

Beyond the bluff, Coast Highway
traffic hums, wrestles with the song
of the sea, that constant cascade
of waves finding their way to shore.

And today, twenty years since your death,
I thought I heard you call my name.

The Sea

The sea
is my woman,
my lover.
This morning
she has little
to offer,
other than
just being there
for me.
Yet, I manage
to embrace
the face
of a few waves
she surrenders.

Tower 22 Ponto Beach

This morning's sky is still a part of the night,
bluer than that lifeguard tower, bluer than
the eyes of a woman I loved in my youth.
Walk with me on this beach, feel sand
damp underfoot, unmarked, smooth
from last night's rain; come with me
to water's edge where the beach
gives way to a long scar of cobbles;
listen to the voice of the ocean, a chaotic
concert of breaking waves; breathe air
baptized in salt water; gather sunlight,
put it in your pocket along with any
shells we might find. And look, beyond
that spindly legged tower, beyond
those eroding coastal bluffs, a faint dab
of white, the Encinas power plant,
smokestack spewing steam.
But what I really want to do while
we are here is climb the blue tower's
ramp, lie on its deck and beg the sun
to give us a sky this blue again tomorrow.

Thursday Morning at Swami's

The concrete bench at Swami's
is cold, damp with dawn.
I sit, careful not to lean against
the bronze memorial plaque
imbedded in its back.
The sea is calm, air heavy
with scents of salt water,
fresh coffee and sunscreen.
Clouds the color of dirty laundry
threaten rain. A scattering of surfers
stare at the horizon. Meaningless swells
march to shore. A fishing boat loiters
out beyond the kelp beds where
a lone dolphin breaks the surface.
On the beach, ropes of rotting seaweed
lie tangled along last night's high tide line.
A swarm of women run at water's edge,
flash of pink shoes, bodies tan and taut.
Sweat glistened arms and legs announce
intentions of eternal youth. A rotund man
in a shirt wet with his effort climbs
the 140 stairs from beach to parking lot
for the third time.
Down the sidewalk two young women,
girls really, push baby strollers.
Conversation is constant, animated,
a flurry of ringed fingers and bright nails.
One has purple highlighted hair,
a butterfly tattoo on her shoulder.
The other hides her face behind
a pair of enormous sunglasses.
A fire breathing dragon hugs her calf.
Enough red ink to stop traffic.
Beneath her blouse, a telltale baby bump.
As they pass, she speaks to her friend,
All I know is, I'll never date a surfer again.

The Same Blue as Your Eyes

I'm drowning
in images of the sea,
waves struggle
against shore,
the sun sets
behind a mock landscape
of clouds.
And in that silent slant
of November sky
I glimpse the same blue
as your eyes.

A December Day at Warm Water Jetty
—for Jeff

Remnants of a waning moon inch toward a ragged horizon,
the sun still low in the east. A whisper of breeze lays a hint
of texture on this vast carpet of ocean. Out beyond small
swells a flotilla of lobster buoys. Nearby, the blue fins of a
snorkel fisherman break the surface and a lone pelican skims
the sea. Gulls rest on the jetty, soon to resume their
scavenger ways. Down the beach two children play in the
sand. Their mother stands at water's edge, her red sweater
like a lighthouse beacon. A boy carrying a surfboard runs
toward the water, conjures up thoughts of my old surf buddy
Jeff. For years we hunted waves together along this beach;
years before the Doctors told him, *Nothing we can do;*
years before I watched his ashes disappear into the blue abyss
of the Pacific. Now, when I paddle out,
                    the water is so crowded with memories
                    I can scarcely tell today from yesterday.

Beach Walk

I walk our favorite beach,
wish with each step
you were at my side.

A small chip from some far-off
mountain, massaged by the sea
for eons, lies half buried in the sand.

It sparkles like your eyes,
its shape similar to a heart.
I am no longer alone.

New Year's Day

Morning air bites at my face.
Beach cobbles rattle
with every attack of waves
that rolls ashore.
The sky is pale blue,
nearly white along the horizon
where the early sun
paints the sea silver.
I walk water's edge,
sand cool, damp
beneath bare feet.
This is the way to begin
a new year. This is the way
it should end someday:
the memory of me, the sea
and an ocean breeze.
And when the current is right
I'll drift north, join my father
when he returns on the tide.

Between Sun & Water

It stands on a bluff above the Pacific
gnarled from decades of coastal winds,
bare branches skeletal against
a sun-drenched sky, not a single leaf
to give hope for greener days.
When I was a child, concerned only
with wading in the blue Pacific,
sand castles & how high I could fly
my kite, this tree was alive with promise.
Now, having grown old together,
this tree & I can only stand between
sun & water, wait for that final sunset.

Summer Wind

I search for remnants
of our hours together
down by the sea.
I find a footprint or two
where we walked. Yet,
just as years have erased
the memory of your face,
tides have rewritten
those steps of our journey.
But the sun has not forgotten
days we worshiped it
even as it faded into
one cloud after another.
I whisper your name
and you come back to me
on the summer wind.

The Hunt

1851—aboard the New Bedford
whaling ship *Benjamin Tucker*

I see the spout, white and ghostly
  like smoke from a signal fire
The very breath of life
  reveals you, betrays you
Do you see us running with the wind
  sails billowed, full, taut against the sky
Can you hear our bow slice the sea
  hear the mast creak and rigging sing
Do you know who we are
  this crew of thirty men and a boy
Do you know we have come
  to chase and slaughter

Will you run before we lower the boats
  or must we first kill your calf
To lure you, bring you near the men
  men eager for the hunt
Men with harpoons and coils of rope
  steel lances and fluke spades
Men with wives and children waiting
  men willing to face you for their share
Will you turn on them in their small boats
  spill them into the sea to die
Will you scream when the harpoon
  rips into your flesh
Then dive and run for the depths
  streaming blood behind
Or let us pull you along side
  and plunge a lance into your heart

Will you cry when the sea runs red
   and you spout blood with every breath
When the end comes, the flurry
   that violent thrashing
And you beat the water with your tail
   and with a final shudder
   roll over on your back
We will slice you into strips
   render your flesh and bones
And the sea will be a pool of blood
   thick and stinking
And we will store you in the hold
   every butchered piece
And you will become
   oil for our lamps
   corset stays for our ladies

Did you imagine you would always be free
   you Grays and Rights and Sperms
   you Blues and Humpbacks
Free to raise your calves
   swim blue waters with your mates

The truth is
When we have squandered all that you were
   blood and bone and breath
   we will be back
We will return for your brothers
We will return for all the others

Beachcombing

An ebb tide leaves behind
those worthless passengers
of storm-tossed waves:
sinewy strands of seaweed,
shells and bits of driftwood.

I think of all I left behind.

I find a stone smooth as a child's
face, flat as the earth before Aristotle.
I skip it across the shallows,
continue my search for something
I won't know until I see it.
That's the way of beachcombing
                              —and love.

Father, I Thought I Saw You

I thought I saw you downtown
in that little cafe where we ate lunch
most days. You were at our favorite table
in the back near the window,
where we would watch the sidewalk
show of tourists and locals.
Yesterday you were in the yard,
in that corner where crows congregate
every morning near that old rose bush
with its scarlet blossoms.
But it was only a whisper of leaves
whipped by the wind, silent in its chaos.
I thought I saw you today at the beach
down along water's edge. You know,
that stretch of shore where I waded in,
let your ashes drift out with the tide
that August day all those years ago.
I thought I saw you today.
But it was just a flash of light
off the ocean, a breaking wave,
the confusion of sea and sunlight.

Sailor's Warning

Beyond the early morning gray
fog lingers in slow retreat
of a rising summer day.

A brush stroke of sky
whispers promises,
paints the morning red.

Winter Afternoon

The one o'clock sun
warms me to the bone
after a late session
in cold January waves.
Out beyond the break
the sea boils with a frenzy
of feeding dolphins. Gulls
circle and swoop down,
join the feast while it lasts.
On the beach, a barefoot
woman walks at water's edge.
She wears a short leather dress
with a long fringe, a large
peace sign on the front.
I make a mental note of what I see.
There may be a poem here.

Blind Boy Mending Fishing Nets
Manzanillo, Mexico

The boy's face reveals little. Yet,
his vacant eyes, always fixed on the sea,
say more than most care to hear.

He is learning the secrets of the sea
from his grandfather and father,
but does not go out in the family boat.

The boy threads a net with an old
wood shuttle, the way his father
and his father's father did before him.

He spends his days on the dock
listening to gulls cry, waves slap against
pilings. These sounds are all he sees.

On the dock a boy mends fishing nets
for his grandfather and father.
But his dreams carry him out to sea.

Saturday Thoughts

I slip into an old sweatshirt, faded shorts,
grab a thermos of coffee, my notebook
and wander off to my favorite beach bench.
The sidewalk is still damp with last night's
rain. Those purple florets along the bluff
cradle tiny droplets in their petals.
Silver clouds sweep in off the ocean.
On the sand a man and young boy toss
a Frisbee. I watch it float between them,
recall a summer Sunday in '74, three friends,
iced beer in a cooler, a Frisbee marathon
that lasted well into evening.
Has it really been forty plus years?
In distant gray waters a dolphin surfaces,
blows a ghost of breath that lingers in still
air, the only evidence it was ever there.
The horizon is being swallowed by fog.
The air chills, becomes thick in my lungs.
I am drowning in thoughts of youth and age.
An old man shuffles past, his small terrier
in a red sweater. Three women strut by
in time to some silent aerobic mantra,
firm bodies displayed in tight shorts, brief tops.
He doesn't give them a glance. My mind
reels with fantasies and I fear that day
when small dogs replace women.

The Gift

I brought you a gift that morning:
two shells I found while walking
that beach we both know,
that beach awash in memories.
But I forgot to offer them
as we talked and shared
small pieces of our lives
across that breakfast table.
I believe it was the contentment
in your eyes, in your voice,
the first time since he left.
So let me tell you of their beauty.
The first has delicate fanned ridges
like a sunburst, making me wonder
if it exploded into creation.
It is delicately thin, nearly translucent,
mottled with the browns and bronze
of the sea. The second is thick, heavy,
with subtle, circular lines of color
like the strata of an ancient rock formation.
I wish you could see them,
beautiful in their complex simplicity,
much like our friendship.

About the author:
Clifton King is an award-winning Southern California poet.
Beach Bum is his eighth book of poetry. He resides in
Carlsbad, California with his wife Katie Rose and two dogs.

Royale Road Publishing

www.ingramcontent.com/pod-product-compliance
Lightning Source LLC
Chambersburg PA
CBHW051731040426
42447CB00008B/1071